BRATZ Xpress Yourself!

Friends, Family, School, and You!

Executive Brand Editor, Charles O'Connor

Used under license by Penguin Young Readers Group. Published by Grosset & Dunlap, a division of Penguin Young Readers Group, 345 Hudson Street, New York, New York 10014. Printed in the U.S.A.

ISBN 0-448-43489-X

A B C D E F G H I J

Contents

Part 3: Super-Cool School!

Part 4: Hey, It's Me!

Hey Girl!

We're all about having a great time. In our new book, "Xpress Yourself!", you'll be able to write all about your one-of-a-kind life! It isn't like a regular diary. You don't have to write in it every day. But when you feel the urge to let it all out, here's the perfect place. We'll help guide you through these pages while you fill in the 411 on friends, family, school, and you! After all, there's only one you—and when you finish this book, there will be no other book like it. That's because there's no one else like you! You're independent! You're unique! So flaunt it! Write down all the wonderful things about you and your world and have a blast doing it!

The Bratz Pack,

Sasha

Cloe

Jade

Yasmin

Meygan

PART 1:
Funkadelic Friends!

Friends...

...see the best in you, even when you're at your worst.

...keep your secrets and share your dreams.

...tell you the truth, even if the truth hurts.

...listen to what you say. They also listen to what you *don't* say.

...stand by you through good times, bad times, and in-between times.

...are like gems—they're priceless!

Fab Friends!

Jade

All of us girls are best friends.
We're a Pack! Who's in your Pack?

My **name** is:

cam

The names of the **pals** in my Pack are:

Meg Alese Nico Isabell
Olabe

This is something **fun** I recently did with my Pack:

we went to the Bridsacowore

We couldn't stop **laughing** when this happened:

web Olabe suite hecendrele
on he momshod

A time when a friend was **totally-cool** to me was when:

We sat bobon thecarpet

These are my **favorite** things to do with my friends:

play at scash. oh the
playgrond

This is the friend I can **tell everything** to:

Nicole

This is the friend I **laugh the most with**:

This is the friend I've **had the longest**:

~~else~~ sofe

This is my **newest** friend:

else

This is the friend who always **stands by me**:

carly

This is the friend who is **most like me**:

Nicole

Fashion Friends!

My buds and I are **into this** look right now:

_____

_____

_____

_____

What's **out** right **now** is:

_____

_____

_____

_____

We mostly agree/disagree on **what looks good**.
(circle one)

This is the latest **cool thing** my girls and I are into:

_____

_____

_____

_____

Stylin' Friends Quiz

Check out this quiz and find your fashion style. Try it with your pals. Do you all agree? Or do you each Xpress your own fashion freedom?

1. Your favorite T-shirt is:
   a. Baby-T with a picture of a cute animal
   b. Dark with a scary image on it
   c. Bright with a bold design
   d. Pastel solid

2. This is what you like to wear to bed:
   a. Boxer shorts and a tank top
   b. Sweats and a T-shirt
   c. Patterned flannel pants with a funky T-shirt
   d. A ruffled nightgown

3. Your idea of a great hair look is:
   a. Braided pigtails
   b. Chunky highlights
   c. Short or spiked
   d. Long and natural

4. Your perfect accessories would be:
   a. An animal-print scrunchie
   b. A spiked choker
   c. A braided rope belt
   d. A silver necklace

5. Your favorite pair of socks would be:
   a. Light blue with little lady bugs
   b. Red-and-black striped pair that go up to the knees
   c. Funky fluorescent with polka dots
   d. Pink argyle

Count up the number of a's, b's, c's, and d's you scored. What letter did you pick most often? Look below to find your fashion style.

A's. If you chose mostly a's, then you are a true fashion diva! You're way chic! Keep on rockin', girlfriend!

B's. If you chose mostly b's, then you're funka-licious! You're always up for an adventure—in fashion and in life!

C's. If you chose mostly c's, then you are one groovy girl! Totally stylin', you never fail to entertain your gal pals anywhere you go!

D's. If you're mostly d's, then you're traditional and way cute. You know what works for you and you flaunt it 'cuz you got it going on!

The Positively Perfect Pal!

Who would be your ideal and perfect pal? Pick the things you like most about your BFFs and write 'em down! You can use one bud as many times as you need to.

My perfect gal-pal would have...

The funky-fresh **fashion** sense of:_____

The hysterical **humor** of:_____

The groovy **dance** moves of: _____

The stupendous **smile** of: _____

The lovely **loyalty** of: _____

The brilliant **brain** of:_____

The amazing **athletic** ability of:_____

The ultra cool **kindness** of: _____

The **super skin** of:_____

The heavenly **hair** of:_____

The knock-out **nails** of: _____

The vivacious **voice** of:_____

And the Award Goes To...

Who would you give these awards to?

Bratz World Award for a Future **World Leader** goes to:

_____

Flaunt It Award for **Funky Fashion** goes to:

_____

Fashion Attitude Award for Most **Self-Confidence** goes to:

_____

Fashion Passion Award for Always **Being Enthused** goes to:

_____

Chic Award for **Super Coolness** goes to:

_____

Independent Award for **Being Unique** goes to:

_____

Look Good, Feel Good Award for **Helpfulness** goes to:

_____

Super-Star Friendships!

The stars say it all! And we're not talking about Hollywood celebs! We're talkin' about astrological stars! See what signs are meant to go together—who knows, you may find a friend in someone you never thought you would have!

 Awesome Aries gets along great with Gemini, Leo, Libra, and Sagittarius pals.

 Tuned-In Taurus gets along great with Cancer, Virgo, Capricorn, and Pisces pals.

 **Genuinely Groovy Gemini** gets along great with Aries, Leo, Libra, and Aquarius pals.

 **Cool Cancer** gets along great with Taurus, Virgo, Capricorn, and Pisces pals.

 Lovable Leo gets along great with Aries, Gemini, Libra, and Sagittarius pals.

Virtuous Virgo gets along great with Taurus, Cancer, Scorpio, and Capricorn pals.

 Funky Libra gets along great with Gemini, Leo, Aquarius and Sagittarius pals.

 Sassy Scorpio gets along great with Cancer, Virgo, Capricorn, and Pisces pals.

 Super-Fun Sagittarius gets along great with Aries, Gemini, Leo, and Aquarius pals.

 Chic Capricorn gets along great with Taurus, Virgo, Scorpio, and Pisces pals.

 Lively Aquarius gets along great with Aries, Gemini, Libra, and Sagittarius pals.

 Playful Pisces gets along great with Taurus, Cancer, Scorpio, and Capricorn pals.

Writing to Faraway Friends!

When Meygan moves away, we'll send IMs, e-mails, and letters to her. Here are some adorable smiles and sayings you can write to your friends!

Writing Short-Cuts for IMs:

LOL – laughing out loud

ROFL – rolling on floor laughing

OMG – oh my gosh

G2G – got to go

ATM – at the moment

BTW – by the way

W/E – whatever

2morrow – tomorrow

buh bye/byez – good-bye

And here are some righteous smiley faces!!

:-p – sticking tongue out

>:-O – yelling/angry

:'(– crying

O.o – confused

:-D – big grin

:-x – oops/not telling

Snail mail is always fun too, because you can read and re-read the awesome letters from your friends! If you decide to use snail mail, try these ideas:

- Cut colorful letters from different magazines, then tape or glue them together to make your own words.
- Dip a narrow paintbrush into lemon juice and write your letter. Let it dry before you send it. It will be invisible, but if you tell your friend to hold the letter up to a light bulb and move it slowly, the letter will become readable.
- Write a long, long letter on a roll of cash-register or adding machine paper (available at most office supply stores). Start writing your letter at the beginning of the roll and keep going until you run out of things to say. Then re-roll the letter and wrap it with a rubber band.

Here We Go!

The Bratz are always on the go! Have you and your pals done something special lately? Write about it here.

Recently, my friends and I **went here**:

We Went to the Soo

This is **what we did**:

We Tried To Catch a Birdd.

Another **special time** we shared was when:

At my Brithday

The **best thing** about this special time was: WEN WE LafEd relly hard.

Pal Snaps!

Use these pages to tape or glue in photos of your pals and you having a blast!

PART 2:
Far-Out Family!
Ten Words That Mean FAMILY

Caring

Comfort

Mother

Father

Brother

LOVE

Nurturing

Support

Understanding

Sister

A Fantastic Family!

All the Info!

These are the **names** of the people in my family:

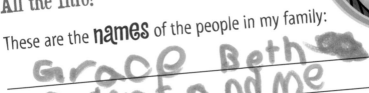

Grace Beth Amanda
robert and me

This is what **we call** my grandparents, aunts, uncles, and cousins:

carol hermam

I think this word best **describes** my family: _____

My family **likes to do** this together: _____

My family sometimes **talks about** this: _____

This is a **place** we like to go together: _____

Our favorite thing to **eat** is: _____

Our favorite **TV show** to watch is: _____

I'm proud that my family is so: _____

Holiday Hubbub!

These are the **holidays** my family celebrates:

_____

_____

My **favorite** holiday is: _____

This is what my family does to **celebrate** that holiday:

_____

_____

On holidays, we sometimes **visit** these people:

_____

_____

Take it from us—traveling with your family on the holidays can get a little crazy. Keep these tips in mind:

DON'T

- Lose your cool. The trip won't last forever.

- Eat too much. Traveling with an upset tummy is never fun.

- Forget to smile.

DO

- Keep your sense of humor.

- Bring along music or an activity to entertain you while traveling.

- Bring your camera!

- Remember that this is a memory in the making, so enjoy yourself.

Where You're At!

Are you the youngest, oldest, or in the middle?
What does your family standing mean?

If you're the **OLDEST**, you always like to do your best. You're a natural leader. You're a take-charge person. And so chic!

If you're a **SECOND**-born, you challenge authority. You stand up for yourself. You're good at ending an argument. And totally funky-fresh!

If you're an **ONLY** child, you're independent. You are comfortable being alone. You speak your mind. And you know how to flaunt it!

If you're the **YOUNGEST**, you're very persuasive. You can be quite charming. You are fun-loving. And very fashion forward!

If you're a **TWIN**, you're good at sharing. You're very cooperative. You are sensitive to the feelings of others. And what great fashion attitude!

If you're **ONE OF MANY**, you're a real team player. You're always helpful. You are able to speak up for what you want. And absolutely cutting-edge!

In my family, here's where I **stand**:

_____

If I had a **choice**,
I'd like to be oldest/youngest/middle/an only child/a twin/one of many
because:

(circle one)

_____

_____

_____

_____

_____

_____

_____

_____

_____

Wild About Pets!

All of us Girls love pets. Here's the space to jot notes on the animals in your family.

We have this/these **pet**(s):

_____

_____

The thing I **love most** about my pet(s) is:

We have a fishe
_____

_____

_____

_____

A **pet** I would love **to have** is a:

_____

_____

I'd **name** it: Jade
_____

_____

Draw a picture of your dream pet here:

Family Fotos

Here's a super-special spot to stick your favorite family fotos. Your family is cool! So flaunt it!

PART 3:
Super-Cool School!

SCHOOL is the place where:

- ☐ you **learn**.
- ☐ you **strive**.
- ☐ you take **risks**.
- ☐ you make **mistakes**.
- ☐ you **connect**.
- ☐ you **grow**.
- ☑ **All** of the **above**!

The 411 on School!

The Bratz Pack loves school. Write all the info on your school right here.

The name of **my school** is:

_____

I'm in the _____ **grade**. My teachers' names are:

_____

_____

_____

The **principal** of our school is:

_____

Other important **people** in our school are:

_____

_____

_____

_____

The most interesting thing we're **learning** about this year is:

_____

_____

_____

_____

Here's what I think of our **cafeteria**:

_____
_____
_____
_____

This is the activity I enjoy most in **gym**:

_____
_____
_____
_____

Next year I hope to get this **teacher**:

Madam ♡ f
_____

What's Your School Style?

The way you sit, answer, walk, and talk in school is uniquely you. What's your school style? Take this quiz and find out.

1. When looking for a seat, you always:

   a. sit right up front.
   b. sit as far back as possible.
   c. think middle is best.

2. If you're caught not paying attention, you:

   a. take a guess at the answer.
   b. get embarrassed and slump down in your seat.
   c. stammer and promise to pay attention from then on.

3. When you know the answer to the teacher's question, you:

   a. shoot your hand into the air eagerly.
   b. don't answer because you don't want to look uncool.
   c. wiggle your fingers.

4. When walking down the hall, you:

   a. walk quickly to your next class.
   b. keep your head down and stroll casually.
   c. smile and wave at everyone.

5. After school, you:

   a. usually stay after for a club or special activity.
   b. like to relax.
   c. have certain activities you enjoy once or twice a week.

What your answers mean:

Mostly A's. Scoring mostly a's gives you A+ school style. You're into everything school has to offer and you get the most out of the hours you spend in school.

Mostly B's. You're cool and casual. Try turning up the energy to get more out of school. You're there, anyway, so be sure to get the most out of the time you put in.

Mostly C's. You're low key, but you get the job done. You might have other interests like sports, music, or art besides regular school subjects. Even a little extra effort helps keep you on track.

After School Is Cool!

What do you like to do when the school day is done?

After school, I participate in these **activities**:

_____

_____

_____

My favorite thing to do **after school** is:

_____

_____

_____

And **this is why**:

_____

_____

_____

Here's a recent after-school **happening** that was really fun:

_____

_____

_____

This is an after-school **activity** I'd like to try next year:

_____

_____

Love Your Locker!

Cams
Locker

It's all about personal style. Design a locker that would Xpress the real you!

School Rules Awards

Xpress yourself! Give out your own school awards here.

The **Funniest** Teacher Award goes to:

_____

The **Toughest** Teacher Award goes to:

_____

The **Sweetest** Teacher Award goes to:

_____

The Most **Creative** Teacher Award goes to:

_____

The All-Time **Favorite** Teacher Award goes to:

_____

The **Funniest** Student Award goes to:

_____

The **Smartest** Student Award goes to:

_____

The Most **Helpful** Student Award goes to:

_____

The Most **Creative** Student Award goes to:

_____

Design Your Own School Award Here:

PART 4:
Hey, It's ME!

My Likes

My Dislikes

My Look

My Goals

You're pretty special—we all are! So many things make you unique. Put them all together and there's no doubt that there's no one else quite like you!

My Style

My Talents

My Sense of Humor

My Dreams

My Personality

My Life

= ME!

What It's Like to Be Me!

Hey, independent, funky girl, tell us all about yourself!

My full **name** is:

_____

My parents named me this **because**:

_____

_____

_____

My **hair** is this color:

_____

This is **how** I like to wear it:

_____

_____

_____

My **eyes** are this color:

_____

I am _____ **feet** and _____ **inches** tall.

I am _____ years **old**.

My **birthday** is_____

Here are some **words that describe me**:
(circle the words that are true for you)

outspoken   good listener
                                                          creative
shy   athletic
                                                          stylish
caring   artistic
                                                          reader
energetic   serious
                                                          carefree
humorous   social
                                                          studious

Other words that describe me:

_____

_____

_____

Here are some **things I really like**:
(circle the words that are true for you)

animals   people
                                                          books
movies   video games
                                                          computers
music   television
                                                          cooking
eating   videos
                                                          dancing
gymnastics   creating art
                                                          sports
fashion   plays
                                                          exercise

Other things I really like are:

_____

_____

_____

Picture This!

Here's the place for drawing a picture of yourself or sticking in a foto!

Primpin' and Pamperin'!

Bratz Beauty is about lookin' good and feelin' good. What do you do to make yourself look and feel great?

Here are some **things I do to look and feel my best:**
(circle the ones that are true for you)

give myself a **manicure**

soak in a **bubble bath**

brush my **hair** until it shines

wear **cologne** or perfume

use moisturizing **cream**

brush and floss my **teeth**

use a **facial mask**

blow-dry my hair

exercise

take a hot **shower**

This also makes me look and **feel great:**

_____

_____

_____

Personality Plus!

We know you're packed with personality! Take the quiz here to figure out your personality style.

1. When you talk to people, you:

    a. look them in the eye.
    b. fold your arms.
    c. move around.

2. When someone says something funny, you:

    a. laugh and nod.
    b. smile gently.
    c. fall against the wall in a hysterical laughing fit.

3. If your pal is wearing an awful-looking outfit, you:

    a. say nothing. Your pal must like it.
    b. avoid your pal that day because you don't know what to say.
    c. kindly suggest that the outfit might not be the best look for your pal.

4. If your friend seems sad, you:

    a. ask your friend what is wrong.
    b. stay close by in case she wants to talk.
    c. ask others if they know what's wrong with your friend.

5. In a large group of people, you:

    a. find a few friends to talk to.
    b. talk to one other person.
    c. keep moving until you've spoken to everyone.

Here's what your answers mean:

Mostly A's. You're a warm, people person. You reach out to people and they can tell you really care about them.

Mostly B's. You're a bit shy. You hold back out of respect for the person's feelings. Don't worry—your friends know you care.

Mostly C's. You're energetic and very outgoing. You're fun to be around. Just be sure to slow down long enough to tune in to the feelings of others.

Electric Funk!

We girls are cutting-edge! That's why we're up on the latest in electronic gizmos and gadgetry. How do these things fit into your world? Write about it here.

These are my favorite **video** games:

_____

_____

_____

These are my favorite **computer** games:

_____

_____

_____

This is my favorite **DVD**:

_____

_____

_____

This is my favorite **music** CD:

_____

This is my favorite **song** on my CD or MP3 player:

_____

These are my favorite types of electronics (circle the one that is true for you):

Video game system

VCR

MP3 player

Phone

Computer

Boombox

TV

Answering machine

Cell phone

Other electronic gadgets I like:

_____

_____

_____

_____

_____

_____

_____

_____

_____

_____

_____

Groovy Guys!

Eitan™, Koby™, Dylan™, and Cameron™ are kickin' cool guys we know! Write about the boys you know.

These are cool **boys** I know: _____

_____

_____

_____

These are some things we **like to do** together: _____

_____

_____

_____

This is a **funny** thing _____ once did:
(name of boy)

_____

_____

_____

This is the most **surprising** thing _____ once did
(name of boy)

_____

_____

_____

The **best part** of having boys as friends is:

_____

_____

_____

_____

_____

_____

Top-Secret Fold-Up Page!

You can write a super-special secret on this page. When you're done writing, cut along the solid line and then fold the page up to the dotted line and tape it closed.

My **super-special secret** is:

_____

_____

_____

_____

- -

_____

_____

_____

_____

_____

_____

_____

_____

DON'T PEEK!
TOP SECRET

DON'T PEEK!
TOP SECRET!

The Boyz Awards!

What boys win your personal awards?

The **Funniest** Boy Award goes to:

_____

The **Nicest** Boy Award goes to:

_____

The **Most Athletic** Boy Award goes to:

_____

The **Hottest** Boy Award goes to:

_____

The Most **Considerate** Boy Award goes to:

_____

The **Easiest to Talk to** Boy Award goes to:

_____

My **Special** Award goes to _____

_____ for being so:

_____

_____

_____

_____

_____

_____

The Name Game!

Did you know that Meygan's nickname is Funky Fashion Monkey? That's because even when she's just hangin' around, she always looks good! Here's a place to write all about your name or nickname.

Everyone **calls me**:

_____

_____

Some people **also** call me:

_____

_____

The **funniest** name anyone calls me is:

_____

_____

This is a **nickname** I'd like to be called:

_____

_____

I think it would be cool to have this **e-mail name**:

_____

_____

If I were a **rock star,** I'd call myself:

_____

_____

The girl's name **I like most** is:

_____

_____

The boy's name that's the **coolest** is:

_____

_____

The Me I Will Be!

We see you lookin' great in the years ahead. What do you think you'll be like?

62

When I'm older, I want to **work as** a:

_____

_____

_____

_____

I do/don't want to get **married** and do/don't want to have **children**.
(circle one)   (circle one)

I want to become very **talented** at doing these things:

_____

_____

_____

I want to **contribute this** to the world:

_____

_____

_____

I want to be **known** as a great:

_____

_____

_____

_____

Predictions!

We just know great things are heading your way!
What do you see coming in the future?

I predict that my **friend** _____ will be doing this:

(friend's name)

_____

_____

_____

I predict that my other **friend** _____ will be doing this:

(friend's name)

_____

_____

_____

I predict that **the world** will be better because of this:

_____

_____

_____

These are my other predictions about the **future**:

_____

_____

_____